Math Basics

Sorting Toys

By Nick Rebman

level 1
little blue readers

www.littlebluehousebooks.com

Little Blue House is distributed by North Star Editions:
sales@northstareditions.com | 888-417-0195

Produced for Little Blue House by Red Line Editorial.

Photographs ©: Shutterstock Images, cover, 4, 7 (top), 7 (bottom), 9, 11 (top), 11 (bottom), 13 (top), 13 (bottom), 15 (top), 15 (bottom), 16 (top left), 16 (top right), 16 (bottom left), 16 (bottom right)

Library of Congress Control Number: 2020900836

ISBN
978-1-64619-170-3 (hardcover)
978-1-64619-204-5 (paperback)
978-1-64619-272-4 (ebook pdf)
978-1-64619-238-0 (hosted ebook)

Printed in the United States of America
Mankato, MN
012021

About the Author

Nick Rebman enjoys reading, walking his dog, and traveling to places where he doesn't speak the language. He lives in Minnesota.

Table of Contents

car

Sorting Toys

We sort the cars by color.

The red cars and

the green cars go in

different spots.

We sort the bricks

by color.

The yellow bricks and

the blue bricks go in

different spots.

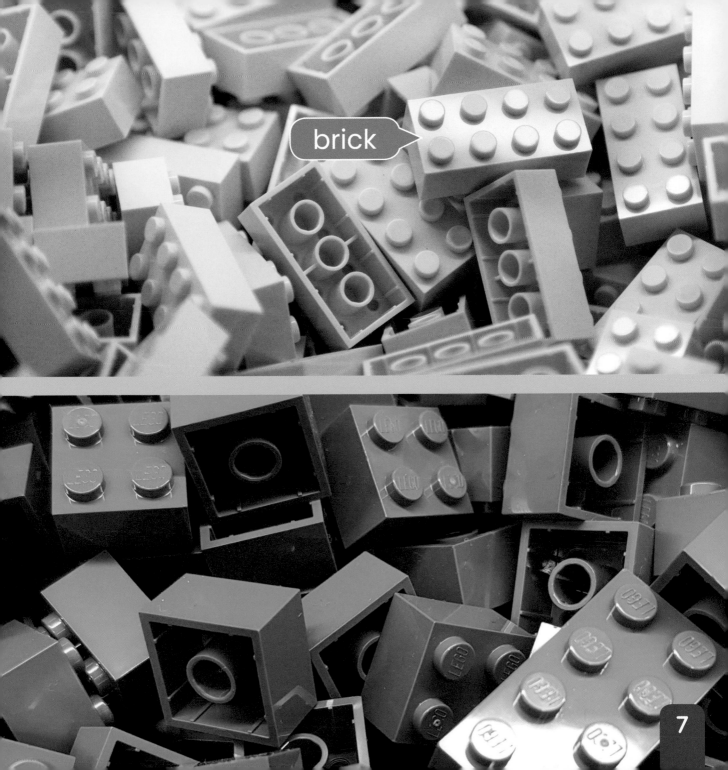

We sort the robots by size. The small robots and the big robots go in different spots.

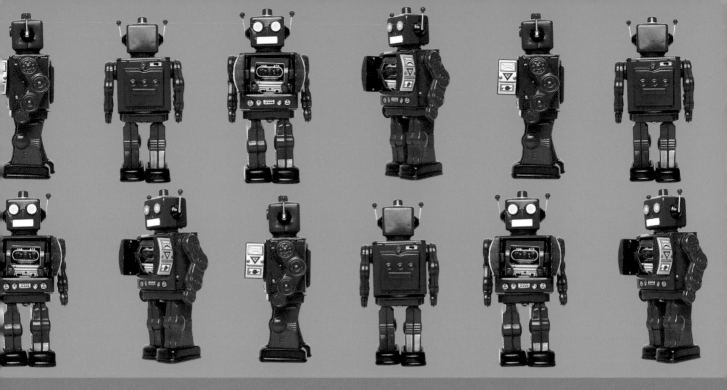

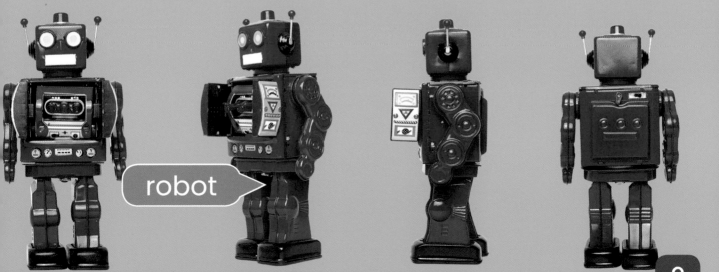

robot

We sort the balls by size. The small balls and the large balls go in different spots.

We sort the blocks by shape.
The triangles and the cubes go in different spots.

triangle

cube

13

We sort the toys by shape. The circles and the stars go in different spots.

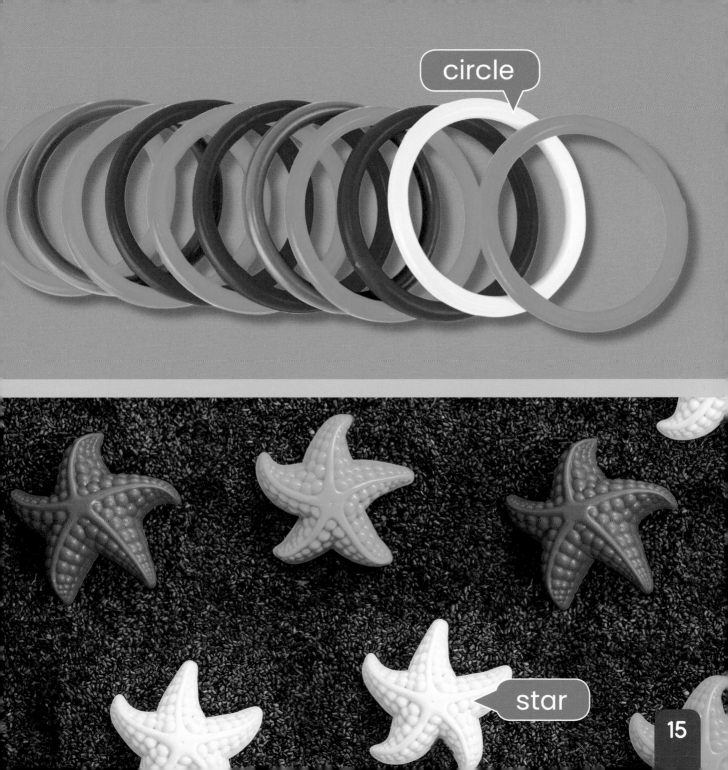

Glossary

brick

robot

car

star

Index